Forest Minibeasts

Lisa Thompson

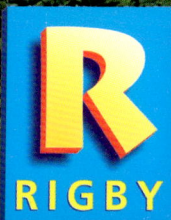

RIGBY

Contents

All Over the Forest

Minibeasts live all over the forest.

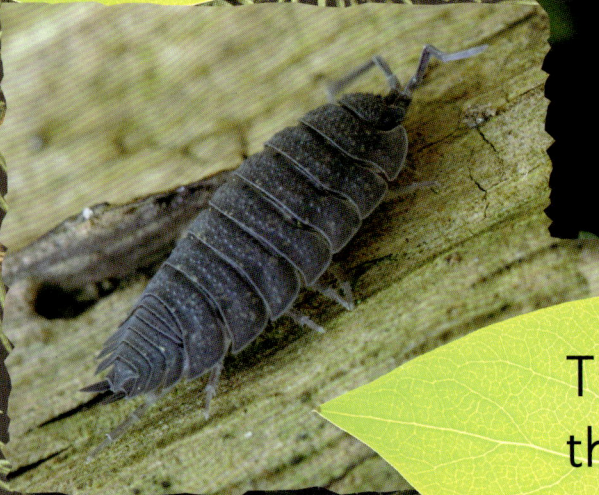

They live on the ground, in the trees and in the air.

On the Ground

Lots of minibeasts live on the ground.

Some minibeasts hunt for food on the ground.

In Tree Trunks

Some minibeasts live inside trees.

eggs

termites

These are termites. They lay their eggs inside tree trunks and in dead wood.

In the Branches

Some minibeasts live in the branches of the trees.

Spiders like to spin their webs in the branches.

On Leaves

Many minibeasts live on leaves in the forest.

Caterpillars like to live on leaves. They eat leaves, too!

In the Air

Many minibeasts fly through the air in the forest.

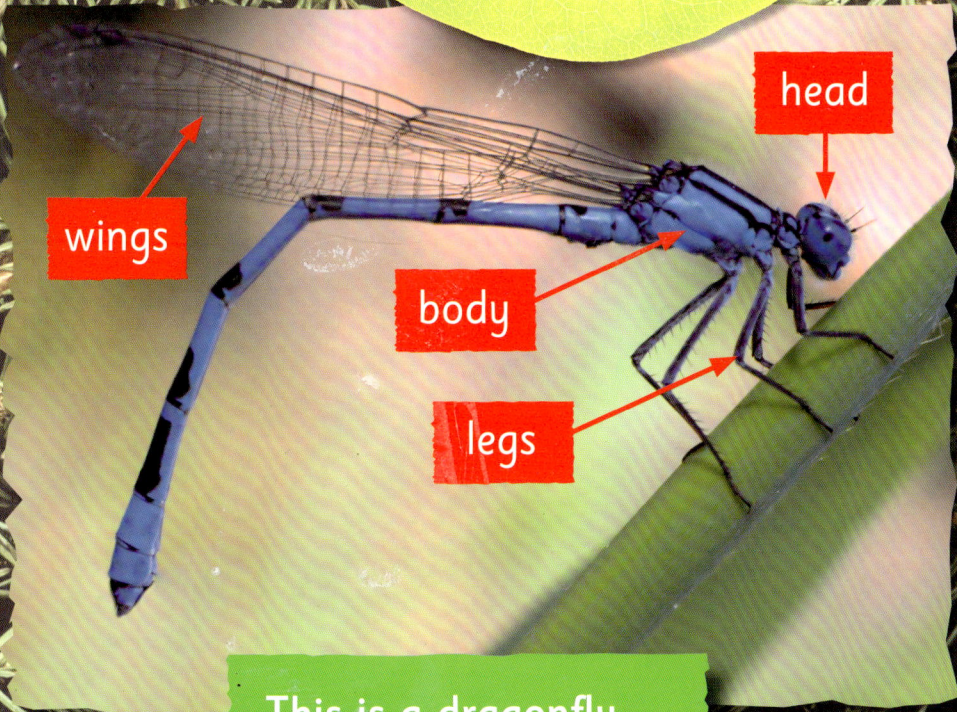

head

wings

body

legs

This is a dragonfly. It has strong wings and a very long body.

What's for Dinner?

Some forest minibeasts like to eat very strange things. Dung beetles eat animal poo.

This dung beetle is walking through the grass, looking for something to eat.

This is a praying mantis. It is a sort of insect.

FACT!

The praying mantis uses its strong front legs to grab other insects.

front legs

The praying mantis grabs other insects and eats them.

11

These caterpillars like to eat plants with green leaves.

Sometimes caterpillars eat so many leaves that the plant dies!

Butterflies and moths feed on nectar from flowers.

butterfly

moth

They stick their long tongues into a flower and suck the nectar out.

How Many Legs?

ants

Ants, bees, flies and butterflies are all insects.

bees

All insects have six legs.

But not all minibeasts are insects.

Some minibeasts have no legs at all, like this earthworm.

Lots of Legs

Centipedes have lots of legs.

A short centipede like this one has 30 legs. A long one can have 350 legs.

Millipedes have even more legs than centipedes.

They have one pair of legs for each part of their body.

FACT!

One millipede can have 375 pairs of legs. That's a lot of legs!

Strong Legs

Grasshoppers have six legs. Their back legs are very strong.

back legs

Grasshoppers use their strong back legs to jump through the air.

Locusts are a type of grasshopper.

They have strong legs for jumping.

FACT!

A big group of locusts is called a swarm. A swarm of locusts can fly hundreds of miles looking for food.

Camouflage

Many minibeasts are very good at hiding in the forest. This is called camouflage.

This moth uses camouflage to hide in the stones.

A stick insect uses camouflage to hide on a tree.

Can you see which is the stick insect, and which is the stick?

A leaf insect can
hide in the leaves.

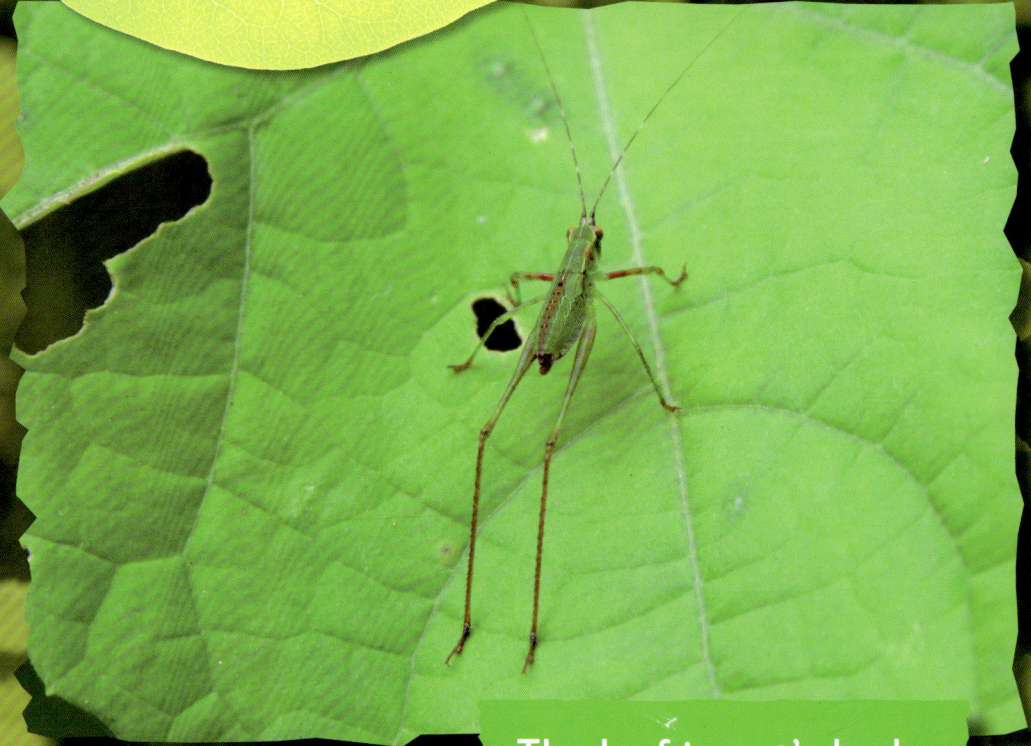

The leaf insect's body
is the same colour
and shape as a leaf.

This mottled sand grasshopper can hide in sandy places.

The grasshopper's body is the same colour as the sand and stones.

Index

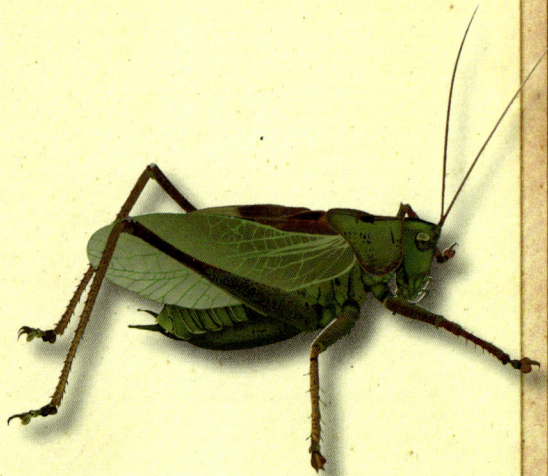